KITTY CORNER

GUIDE TO KITTENS

By Ellen Miles

SCHOLASTIC INC.

No part of this publication may be reproduced, stored in a retrieval system, or transmitted in any form or by any means, electronic, mechanical, photocopying, recording, or otherwise, without written permission of the publisher. For information regarding permission, write to Scholastic Inc., Attention: Permissions Department, 557 Broadway, New York, NY 10012.

ISBN 978-0-545-48434-3

12 11 10 9 8 7 6 5 4 3 2 1   13 14 15 16 17 18/0

Printed in the U.S.A.   40

First printing, January 2013

Book design by Kay Petronio

CONTENTS

INTRODUCTION

A cat wants food and water, sunshine, safety, company, a gentle touch, something to play with, and a cozy place to sleep. A person wants a sweet friend, a funny companion, a soft, furry head to scratch, a little animal to take care of. The first step is to find each other. The steps after that include getting used to each other, finding the right food and other supplies, setting up your house for your new pet, getting to know each other's ways, and solving problems. This book was written to help you go through the steps to make a forever home for a cat or kitten.

Planning for a Kitten or Cat

YOU long for a cat of your own, and you know you will take the best possible care of your kitty. So what are you waiting for? Not so fast! This kind of decision involves everyone and everything in your home.

HERE ARE SOME QUESTIONS TO DISCUSS WITH YOUR FAMILY, AND SOME ADVICE ABOUT EACH TOPIC.

What Kind of Cat Do You Want?

- ☐ domestic shorthair:
  - ☐ solid color
  - ☐ tabby (striped)
  - ☐ calico (spotted female)
  - ☐ tuxedo (black and white)
- ☐ fancy breed:
  - ☐ Maine coon
  - ☐ Persian
  - ☐ Siamese
  - ☐ Manx

☑ ANY KIND OF CAT!

Can you afford cat food and veterinary bills?

Get advice from a local animal shelter or veterinarian about costs.

Is anyone allergic to cats?

If cats make you cough or sneeze, if they give you asthma or make your eyes water, you could be allergic. If you're not sure, get a doctor's advice before adopting a cat.

Does everyone get along with cats?

Consider babies and little children, people who are scared of cats, or people who dislike them. Cats are not for everybody.

Can you handle this particular cat?

Is he a long-haired cat? An indoor cat? An outdoor cat? Do you plan on getting more than one cat? Thinking about your home situation and your family's needs will help you answer these questions.

If you have a certain cat in mind, try to learn about him and talk about his needs with your family. Some cats need to be the only cat or the only pet. Some don't do well around children, or groups of people, or noise. Find out all you can and take the time to make a good decision with your family.

Another cat may be best for you. Another home may be best for the cat you have in mind. Or you may have to make some changes to create a happy forever home.

DUCHESS

Mia wasn't sure that Duchess would like being stuck in one room. Duchess was the type of cat who liked to roam around and find the most comfortable places to perch. —Duchess

FROM THE KITTY CORNER

OTIS

In Otis, Pete wants to adopt Otis, but his noisy band practice frightens the little kitten. Pete tries to figure out what he can do to help Otis feel comfortable.

STEP 2

ADOPT ME

Finding a Kitten or Cat

NOW that your family has decided to adopt a cat . . .

WHAT EQUIPMENT DO YOU NEED? AND WHAT WILL YOU NEED TO DO? HERE COMES YOUR NEW KITTY OR CAT! NOW IS THE TIME TO GET READY.

Where Can You Find Your New Pet?

- Take in a lost or stray kitten or cat.
- ☑ Visit a shelter.
- Answer an ad to adopt a kitten or cat.
- Ask your local veterinarian if he or she knows of a cat who needs a home.
- Buy a kitten at a pet shop that features pets from shelters. *But be careful—pet shops often do a poor job of caring for animals and do not promote responsible breeding. Most pet shops are not good places to find pets.*

CALLIE

A pink nose and white whiskers appeared from behind the paper-recycling can. A kitten! It really was a kitten! —Callie

212

Now that your family has decided to get a cat, be on the lookout for one to adopt. Cats and kittens may arrive at your door in all kinds of ways. Maybe you'll be outside your house and spy a stray kitten who's on her own. Helping her to get the food and shelter that she needs may be a good idea.

Or you may find a kitten someone has abandoned. Sometimes families decide to look for a cat or kitten at a shelter. Internet sites and newspapers often list animals for adoption. You might hear about a new litter of kittens in your neighborhood. Or a vet might tell you about a family who is moving or going through other changes and looking for a home for their pet.

FREE KITTENS 2 1

Here it is, the moment you've dreamed of: Someone invites you to take in a kitten or cat for a little while, or maybe even forever. Here comes your new cat or kitten! Now is the time to get ready.

OTIS

Michael and Mia both gasped when a small orange kitten appeared, cowering in the creases of a hamburger wrapper. He looked scrawny and hungry, and he trembled as he stared up at them with big, round yellow eyes. —Otis

Meeting Basic Needs

A full belly, a warm place to sleep, a healthy body, and love.

WHAT IS YOUR NEW CAT LIKE? IS HE A PURRER? IS SHE A CHASER? A MEOWER? A HUNTER? A SCRATCHER? A GOOFBALL? A GOOD EATER? A PICKY EATER? A SCAREDY-CAT? A BOLD CAT?

No matter what kind of cat he is, you want to make him as comfortable and confident as possible, as fast as possible. Note that it's important to take a found animal to the veterinarian before bringing him into your home. (For more on vets, see Step 4.)

A found cat may need a bath and/or brushing. You'll need an adult to help with this; one person can hold the cat while the other washes or brushes him.

For a bath, you can line the kitchen sink with a towel, and add two or three inches of warm water. Use a plastic cup to gently pour water over the cat, saving the head and face for last. The cat will not like being set down in deep water, and probably won't put up with the sprayer hose, either. He may struggle to get away, and try to scratch or bite. Be careful! Let him go if he really seems upset. Wash him with baby shampoo or pet soap, rinse, and gently dry.

23

For tough cleaning problems, hard-to-handle cats, or terrible tangles, consider taking your cat to the vet or a groomer.

OTIS

"It's okay, boy. We'll make this nice and quick. I just need to get you wet so I can wash some of this crusty stuff off you." Jackson and Michael had read that cats rarely need baths, since they clean themselves, but Otis was really dirty. — Otis

Every cat or kitten needs:

- [ ] a litter box, liner bag, scoop, and litter

- [ ] a food dish and a water dish, food, and water

- [ ] a blanket or cat bed

FROM THE KITTY CORNER

OTIS

The Battelli family always feeds their foster cats in a private little nook by the refrigerator. A cat who isn't touched or bothered by people or other animals will eat better and feel better.

Food and Water

A cat needs her own food and water dishes. They should be washed regularly—just like your own dishes! Place them in a quiet area, out of the way of other pets and people's feet. The water dish should be kept full of clean, cool water.

What about milk?

After about twelve weeks of age, which is the best age for a kitten to be adopted, cats don't need milk for good nutrition. Some cats are lactose intolerant, which means that milk bothers their digestive system. Water is best.

Some cats eat wet food (from cans). Others eat only dry food. Many prefer a combination. It may take some experimenting to find the mix that your cat likes best. For starters, ask the advice of the previous caretaker. What has she been eating so far? Which foods, and how much?

Lots of people feed their cats table scraps, such as chicken or fish. However many vets and other cat experts believe that cats shouldn't be fed "people food."

When you take your cat for her first veterinarian visit, ask the vet's advice on the best feeding plan for your new pet.

Kittens need small meals up to five or six times a day. Fully grown cats are fed twice, morning and evening. Some cats hog all the food down right away, while others eat a little at a time.

What about cat treats?

Use them only as special treats to reward your cat for good behavior. A cat can become unhealthy if she gets too many treats.

You'll know your cat or kitten is doing well if she seems to be growing, has shiny, healthy fur, likes to play, and has no bathroom problems.

CALLIE

Where am I? This is a new place. It looks new, and it smells new. And there are so many people! —Callie

DOMINO

Domino rolled over on his back and stretched out. —Domino

Cat Body Language

:paw: **PURRING:** shows contentment or "this is okay" (some cats purr at the vet's office, even when they're nervous)

:paw: **STRETCHING OR ROLLING:** cat is confident, relaxed

RUBBING AGAINST YOU WITH CHEEK OR BODY: cat likes you and wants to mark you as her own (cats have scent glands in their cheeks to mark you with)

MEOWING: cat is calling or complaining or begging

TAIL TWITCHING: cat is alert or cautious

TAIL WAGGING: shows annoyance

EARS LAID BACK: shows fear or dislike

HISSING: cat is warning or threatening

Litter Box

A litter box with a plastic liner bag makes for easy, hands-clean disposal. You don't need to dump all the litter every day. Aim for once a week. Daily, use the litter scoop to remove big clumps into a closed garbage container.

Some cats kick the litter out of the litter box as they try to cover things up. For easy cleanup, the litter box can be placed in a bathtub or shower.

How do you get a kitten or cat to use the litter box?

After your cat is done eating, put him in the litter box. He might get the idea right away. Or you could use a stick to scratch in the litter to show him "this is the place to scratch around." Cats usually scratch litter over their pee or poop, so

this helps them get the message about the litter box. Some cat owners advise holding the cat's paw and scratching in the litter.

If your cat jumps out, put him back in. Do this gently, while talking quietly and patting your cat. After he pees or poops, praise him and pet him.

Repeat this until you're sure your cat knows what the litter box is for.

Never yell at or hit your cat for making a mistake. Instead, be gentle and patient. With support and kindness, your cat will learn what to do.

Collar

If your cat goes outside, you'll want to give her a collar. Get a tag made with your name and phone number, or write this information on the collar in permanent marker. You should be able to slip your pinky between the collar and the cat's neck to make sure it's tight enough not to catch on fences and bushes, but loose enough so the cat can breathe easily.

Some people put bells on their cats' collars to warn birds of their approach—but others say this interferes with a cat's balance.

Scratching Post

Cats often sharpen their claws. Some scratch on carpets or furniture, and their claws can really tear things up. You can buy a scratching post at a pet shop, or you can make your own out of an old piece of carpet and a board. (Check the Internet with your parents for how-tos.) Some people have their cat's claws removed to keep them from scratching, but this can be painful—and declawed cats must never be allowed outdoors.

Sleeping Spot

Even if your cat likes to sleep on your bed or couch, he may like having his own special bed in a warm,

private spot. You can make a bed from an old pillow or blanket, or find one at a pet shop. Consider putting this bed on a sunny shelf or windowsill where the cat can perch unseen.

Cat Carrier

Borrow or buy a cat carrier to get your cat home from the shelter or to the vet, the groomer, or a cat-sitter's house. If your cat gets comfortable with the carrier, he may want to hang out in it to get some private time, even when he's not traveling.

FROM THE KITTY CORNER

DUCHESS

When Duchess first comes home with Mia, she stays inside her carrier until she feels comfortable with the Battellis.

STEP 4

Vet Check

EVERY

pet needs a vet!

Things to Talk to the Vet About:

- ☐ vaccination shots
- ☐ health checkup
- ☐ spaying or neutering
- ☐ getting a microchip
- ☐ trimming claws (not declawing)
- ☐ planning emergency care
- ☐ rabies shot and certificate
  (required in many states)

FROM THE KITTY CORNER

OTIS

The Battelli family takes every foster pet to see Dr. Bulford at Wags and Whiskers. The cost of veterinarian visits is an important thing to consider before getting a cat.

CALLIE

With a mighty leap, Callie burst out of the carrier and landed on Dr. Bulford's examination table. "You're a frisky one, aren't you?" the vet said. "I won't hurt you. I just need to look at that paw." —Callie

46

First, it's good to know that your pet is healthy, getting enough to eat (but not too much), and growing well.

The vet can check your cat for worms, ticks, and fleas. You should be sure this is done before bringing a new cat into your house.

The vet can also tell you what shots your cat needs to keep from getting sick. She can schedule shots and spaying or neutering for kittens, who must reach a certain age before they can be "fixed" so they can't have kittens of their own. And she can give you advice on daily care and any problems you might have with your new cat.

There are two other important things your vet can do for your cat: prevent loss and plan for emergencies.

A vet can place a tiny microchip in your cat's body during a quick operation in the office. The microchip holds information about you so that if someone finds your cat, they can let you know. It also sends out a radio signal so that you can find your cat yourself.

A vet can also help you put together a plan for emergency medical care for your cat: whom to call or where to go if your cat is hurt or gets sick when the vet isn't available to help.

veterinary care

Fun, Love, and a Place of Her Own

LET'S hear some purring, please!

Your kitten or cat is home. She has a comfortable place to sleep, plenty of food and water, and a litter box. What's next?

Many cat owners keep their cats in a limited space during the first few days. You can make a cozy sleeping space for a cat in a bedroom, bathroom, or spare room. Be sure to include an eating place and a litter box.

Getting to know a new home's sounds and smells may be easier for a cat or kitten who is kept in one room. And a timid cat or kitten can get lost—or overwhelmed—in a whole house or apartment. Once you all get used to each other, open the door.

In the meantime, you can go in to visit your new cat, pet her, feed her, teach her to use the litter box, and play with her.

If there is another pet in the house, keep them separate for a few days while they have a chance to smell, hear, and eventually see each other. Before they meet, switch toys or a piece of their bedding to give them a closer sniff.

When you do get two cats together for the first time, get someone else to help you play with them with strings or shoelaces.

Playing side by side may distract them and help them get used to each other. Let them have their separate spaces until you are sure they're comfortable together.

DUCHESS

"Where's Boone?" Mia asked, looking around for the kitten.

"He's in the bathroom," Catherine said, motioning to a nearby door. "When you introduce two cats, it's best to do it slowly so they can get used to each other. We wouldn't want them to start off with a fight." —Duchess

55

Some cat experts say the best advice is this: Leave the cat alone!

They say that cats will let you know how much attention they want. A cat who comes to you or jumps in your lap wants to be petted or cuddled. A cat who attacks your shoes or hair wants to play.

On the other hand, a cat who jumps down from your lap, runs away to hide under the bed, scratches, or bites is letting you know that he needs more time to get used to you or doesn't want the kind of attention you are giving him. Be gentle, understanding, and patient.

The kitten nipped at Michael's hand again and looked him in the eye. Michael knew the kitten didn't mean to hurt him, but he was definitely trying to tell him something.

"Okay, okay, I'll put you down," Michael said. —Domino

You probably won't have to coax your kitten to play with you! Many older cats like to play, too. Cats love strings or curly ribbon, furry things or things that move in a jerky manner, like a bug or mouse they might catch in the wild. Watch for strings or wires that might entangle or shock a cat, and beware of small items your cat could choke on.

Some cats enjoy catnip. You can try to grow a catnip plant, especially if you see your cat investigating plants.

CATNIP

SOME WARNINGS:

Certain houseplants can be poisonous to cats. Ask your parents to help you learn whether your houseplants are safe for cats. Also, don't encourage your cat or kitten to attack your hand or fingers. That teaches a lesson that could be painful for you or someone else.

Kitty Fun

 shoelace or ribbon

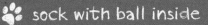 small ball

 stuffed mouse

sock with ball inside

box or paper bag (no plastic bags!)

Caring for a pet can help you learn to understand what someone else needs, and to put your pet's needs first. Here's wishing you health and happiness with your forever kitty.

FROM THE KITTY CORNER

OTIS

Mia and Michael's family helps match cats and kittens with people who want them and who will care for them. They know that a safe home is the right place for a cat to be, and are ready to keep the cat for as long as it takes to find the right forever family.

STEP 7

Keeping Your Cat or Kitten Safe

PROTECTING

your new pet.

Not every cat will be happy indoors. Say your kitten was born outside in a barn, garage, or other open area. She may be used to coming and going, and could feel trapped inside a house. Another, older cat, whose last owner let him out, may get cranky if kept inside. And a cat who has never been out may be terrified if left in the yard.

What should you let your cat do about the inside/outside question? The answer depends on the cat, and on how and where your family lives. It may be safer and more convenient—not to mention easier on wild birds—to make your cat a house cat.

A cat can be walked on a leash, put outside in a pet crate or dog run, or let onto a screened porch. If you let your cat out loose, go with her at first, so that she learns to stay near the house and come back to the door when she wants to come in or when she is called.

You can call a cat by calling her name, by meowing, or opening a can of cat food—music to a cat's ears! When the cat comes, give her a pat or a treat. Praise and rewards are great ways to get a pet to do the right thing.

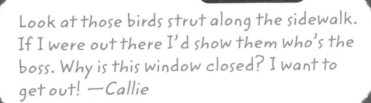

CALLIE

Look at those birds strut along the sidewalk. If I were out there I'd show them who's the boss. Why is this window closed? I want to get out! —Callie

Lost Kitten!

Experts say that "lost" cats are often found very near their homes, hiding. A cat who has been scared by a dog, a truck, or something else may hunker down and hide for several days, even though he can hear his owner calling.

To find your cat, try thinking like a small animal. Get low to the ground and look for a hiding place. While you're there, look for clues like tufts of hair or paw prints that might lead you to your cat's hiding place.

You will also want to put up some posters showing a photograph of your pet. A cat may hide or run someplace unfamiliar, then stay put because he's afraid. Someone may have an eye out for a LOST CAT sign. Make sure to let your veterinarian know about your lost cat, and call the local police and animal control officer.

Best of all, have your cat microchipped [see page 48]. This lets your vet help you track your cat, and can provide your contact information to whoever finds him.

If Your Pet Dies

Even with the most loving care, bad things can happen. Cats or kittens can get sick or hurt and not get better. When you own a cat, focus on giving her the best life possible. Then, if something happens, you will know that your pet was happy. It's a sad fact of life that cats and other animals don't live as long as people. And sometimes kids have to go through the death of a pet.

Lots of people hold and touch their pets after they die. This helps them to say good-bye. Pets can be buried in your yard, or a vet can have them cremated so you can bury or keep the ashes. You can make or buy a gravestone or other memorial.

After your pet dies, share photographs and stories with your family, and treasure your memories together. After a while, you may open your heart and home to a new pet.

DUCHESS

A nice, easy afternoon on the couch.
I hope I can stay here. —Duchess

GLOSSARY

abandon: to leave somewhere or someone and not return

breed: a particular kind of plant or animal; to mate and give birth to young

groomer: a professional who washes, trims, and brushes pets

litter: a number of baby animals that are born at the same time to the same mother

neuter: to make a male animal unable to produce young

rabies: a disease that is often fatal (deadly) to animals and people

shelter: a place where an animal that is not wanted can stay

spay: to make a female animal unable to produce young

WEBSITES

This book is just a start. There's always more to learn about cats! Check out these websites, and don't forget that your library probably has lots of books about cats and cat care.

The American Society for the Prevention of Cruelty to Animals (ASPCA): Cat Care:
aspca.org/home/pet-care/cat-care

Animal Planet: Cat Health 101: 10 Tips for Bringing a New Kitten Home:
animal.discovery.com/healthy-pets/cat-health-101/10-tips-for-bringing-a-new-kitten-home.html

Cornell University College of Veterinary Medicine: Choosing and Caring for Your New Cat:
www.vet.cornell.edu/fhc/brochures/newcat.html

Humane Society of the United States: Bringing Your New Cat Home:
humanesociety.org/animals/cats/tips/
bringing_new_cat_home.html

Humane Society of the United States: Cat Care Essentials:
humanesociety.org/animals/cats/tips/cat_
care_essentials.html

Petfinder: Bringing Home a New Cat:
petfinder.com/after-pet-adoption/
bringing-home-new-cat.html

Purina: Welcoming Your New Kitten:
purina.com/kitten-care/life-at-home/
welcomingyournewkitten.aspx

WebMD Healthy Pets: Bonding with Your New Kitten:
pets.webmd.com/cats/guide/bonding-with-
your-new-kitten

INDEX

PHOTO CREDITS